GUIDE TO GREEK MYTHOLOGY

Don Nardo

ReferencePoint
Press®

San Diego, CA

About the Author

Classical historian and award-winning author Don Nardo has written numerous acclaimed volumes about ancient civilizations and peoples. They include more than three dozen overviews of the mythologies of the Sumerians, Babylonians, Egyptians, Greeks, Romans, Persians, Celts, Norse, and others. Nardo, who also composes and arranges orchestral music, lives with his wife, Christine, in Massachusetts.

© 2022 ReferencePoint Press, Inc.
Printed in the United States

For more information, contact:
ReferencePoint Press, Inc.
PO Box 27779
San Diego, CA 92198
www.ReferencePointPress.com

Picture Credits:
Cover: Svietlieisha Olena/Shutterstock

6: delcarmat/Shutterstock
10: Sven Hansche/Shutterstock
14: AKG Images/Newscom
17: Bridgeman Images
23: Depositphotos

26: The Stapleton Collection/Bridgeman Images
30: © Look and Learn/Bridgeman Images
36: ZU_09/iStock
39: © Look and Learn/Bridgeman Images
43: © Christie's Images/Bridgeman Images
46: Bridgeman Images
53: © Archives Charmet/Bridgeman Images

LIBRARY OF CONGRESS CATALOGING-IN-PUBLICATION DATA

Names: Nardo, Don, 1947- author.
Title: Guide to Greek mythology / by Don Nardo.
Description: San Diego, CA : ReferencePoint Press, Inc., 2022. | Includes
  bibliographical references and index.
Identifiers: LCCN 2021023646 (print) | LCCN 2021023647 (ebook) | ISBN
  9781678202385 (library binding) | ISBN 9781678202392 (ebook)
Subjects: LCSH: Mythology, Greek.
Classification: LCC BL783 .N37 2022 (print) | LCC BL783 (ebook) | DDC
  398.20938--dc23
LC record available at https://lccn.loc.gov/2021023646
LC ebook record available at https://lccn.loc.gov/2021023647

CONTENTS

Ancient Greece (Circa 500 BCE)

Tales That Instilled Fear of the Divine

The timeless myths of the ancient Greeks, which they called *muthoi*, were filled with colorful characters, some divine, others human or monstrous. One of the most notorious of those characters was Tantalus, a mortal son of Zeus, leader of the Greek gods. The heinous crime that Tantalus committed set in motion a series of compelling, chilling events that affected entire generations of his descendants. That chain of incidents also graphically illustrated the incredible power the gods wielded over humans and how deeply belief in and fear of the gods affected ancient Greek life and customs.

The Dastardly Scheme

The trouble that Tantalus caused was a major surprise to the gods. When he was a child and young man, they all adored him, and at their invitation he frequently dined with them in their splendid palaces atop Greece's highest peak — Mount Olympus. What those immortal beings did not know was that he actually resented them and secretly dreamed of finding a way to humiliate them.

Finally, Tantalus conceived a dastardly scheme. His plan was to transform the supposedly superior deities into a

band of depraved cannibals. First, he cruelly killed his own son, Pelops, and then sliced the body into pieces, which he combined with vegetables and spices to create a hideous stew. Next, Tantalus asked several of the Olympians to dinner at his own house. They happily arrived, and their host placed bowls containing the awful main dish before them.

At that tense moment, however, it was Tantalus's turn to be surprised. Employing their highly developed sense of smell, the divinities immediately realized what was in the stew, and in a fit of disgust and anger they turned on Tantalus in a fury. His punishment was severe. In the great epic poem, the *Odyssey*, the

In one myth, Tantalus (pictured) suffered torment in the underworld. After he tried but failed to fool the gods, they surrounded him with water he could never drink and fruit that was always just out of reach.

Greek poet Homer described the wrong-doer's fate in the dark depths of the underworld. Tantalus, he said, stood in a pool of water. But he was never able to drink any of the precious liquid because "whenever he stooped in his eagerness to lap the water, it disappeared."[1] Thus, the sinner remained unbearably thirsty for all eternity.

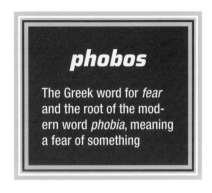

phobos

The Greek word for *fear* and the root of the modern word *phobia*, meaning a fear of something

As terrible as that penalty was, it was not enough to appease the still fuming Olympians. They also inflicted a far-reaching curse on Tantalus's family line, beginning with his grandsons, Thyestes and Atreus, who were compelled to commit horrifying acts. Atreus slew Thyestes's two children, made a stew from them, and served it to their father. Next, the curse struck Atreus by passing to his own son, Agamemnon, ruler of the kingdom of Mycenae. Agamemnon's wife, Clytemnestra, murdered him; after which their son, Orestes, killed her to avenge his father's slaughter.

Overcome with fear (*phobos*) and agony (*agonia*), Orestes traveled from one Greek kingdom to another, ever worried that the gods would strike out at him next. Eventually, he arrived in Athens, whose divine patron was Zeus's daughter, Athena, goddess of war and wisdom. There, Orestes went to

agonia

The Greek word for *agony*

her temple and begged for her mercy. By this time, most of the gods felt that the family had suffered enough, and Athena forgave him. With a wave of her majestic hand, she thereby lifted the curse that had devastated generations of Tantalus's offspring.

Deities of Immense Power

That the gods could so easily impose and remove the overwhelming urge in humans to destroy their own kinfolk was a testament to those deities' immense power. The ancient Greeks not only believed the gods were real but also accepted that those beings could at any moment utterly destroy humanity if they chose to. The fifth-century-BCE Greek poet Pindar summed up that idea, saying of the gods and humans, "From a single mother we both draw breath. But a difference of power in everything keeps us apart."[2]

One result of that stark reality was that the Greeks regarded those deities with a mixture of fear and respect. As the late, great scholar C.M. Bowra put it, "In their undecaying strength and beauty, the gods have something denied to humans, which makes them objects of awe and wonder. The Greek sense of the holy was based much less on a feeling of the goodness of the gods than on a devout respect for their incorruptible beauty and unfailing strength."[3]

It is hardly surprising that the feelings of awe and esteem the Greeks had for their gods, which the myths perpetuated in succeeding generations, strongly affected Greek beliefs and social customs. Those ancient tales "played a considerable part in the education of Greek youth," Bowra wrote. "But more important and more influential was their indirect impact"[4]—namely, the way they shaped human values. Indeed, the Greeks learned numerous moral lessons from their myths.

Such lessons were for the Greeks more important than whether the events depicted in the myths had actually happened. Most people assumed that a majority of those events *had* occurred, but highly educated Greeks suspected that at least some aspects of the stories were mere fables. Yet that did not detract from their beauty and value for moral instruction. Hence, those tales continued to pass from one generation to another, losing none of their luster as they did. Moreover, that process ended up greatly outlasting ancient Greek civilization itself. "In the course of being handed down from father to son," scholar Philip Mayerson points out, some likely real historical events of the dim past were embellished with some "highly imaginative detail, until they were turned into the fascinating stories which have survived to this day."[5]

CHAPTER ONE

Origins of the Greek Myths

The fifth-century-BCE Athenian scholar and philosopher Plato once said that a myth is the story of an event that occurred in the past, "as the poets tell us." Many people believe it really happened, he pointed out; however, such an event "never happened in our time and I don't know that it could."[6] For Plato and most other ancient Greeks, therefore, myths had two distinguishing traits. First, they described things that took place in the distant past. Second, those events could not happen in the mundane present, which implies they contained certain fantastic or miraculous elements peculiar to those *archaeos*, or very ancient, eras. For the Greeks, a principal hallmark of those fantastic times consisted of the gods descending to earth and interacting with people. Also typical of that long-ago age were exploits of bigger-than-life human heroes.

archaeos

The Greek word for *ancient*, from which come the words *archaic* and *archaeology*

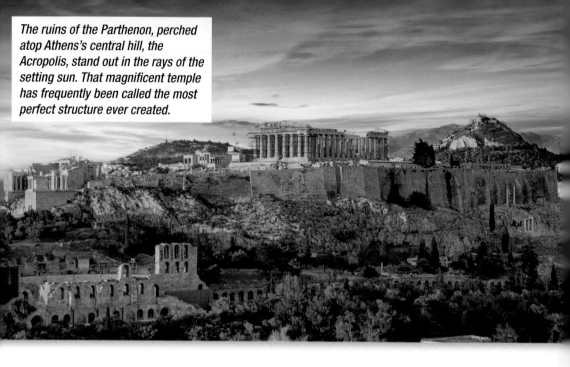

The ruins of the Parthenon, perched atop Athens's central hill, the Acropolis, stand out in the rays of the setting sun. That magnificent temple has frequently been called the most perfect structure ever created.

By the time of Plato and his contemporaries, who lived in what modern historians call Greece's Classic Age (ca. 500–323 BCE), the myths were already very old. They formed a great corpus, or collection, of colorful tales that had been passing from one generation to another for a very long time. Thus, the classical Greeks, who invented democracy, philosophy, science, and the theater and fashioned the majestic Parthenon temple, did *not* also create their mythology. Rather, they inherited it.

Lacking a Clear Idea of History

That inheritance was crucial to the classical Greeks because the myths served several important functions. They were highly entertaining, of course. But because those tales involved the gods, they were also part of the religion that Greeks everywhere then shared. Moreover, a number of the myths described events that the classical Greeks assumed had actually happened, making them in a loose sense historical documents. Finally, many myths were morality tales that defined right and wrong and justice and injustice, and therefore they became integral to the education of each new generation of Greeks.

The burning question—one the classical Greeks were never able to answer precisely—was, Where had the wondrous corpus of myths come from? Plato and the other thinkers of his time did their best to answer that question. Their theory, which became an article of faith to Greeks of all walks of life, was that the heroes of the myths had been real people. Likewise, the Trojan War, in which some early Greeks sacked the city of Troy, had been an actual event. The classical Greeks came to call that primeval period in which the gods supposedly regularly walked among humans the Age of Heroes.

Peoples of Greece's Bronze Age

One serious problem the Greeks had with this theory was that they lacked a clear idea of how long in the past the supposed heroic age had taken place. For that reason, they were never able to determine for certain how old the myths were. Today, by contrast, scholars have a far clearer vision of the march of history. In large part this is because they have the benefit of a science that did not exist in ancient times—archaeology, the excavation and study of past civilizations. In the past couple of centuries, archaeologists have managed to fairly firmly date Greece's heroic period to roughly a millennium before Plato's time. More or less, the Age of Heroes matches up with Greece's late Bronze Age, lasting from about 1600 to about 1100 BCE. (The term *Bronze Age* denotes that people then employed weapons and tools made of bronze, a mixture of copper and tin.)

Something else that the classical Greeks did not know, and that archaeologists do, is that during the late Bronze Age, Greece was occupied by an earlier civilization. It featured two separate peoples, each in control of a distinct portion of the Greek sphere. On the one hand, the large island of Crete and nearby Aegean Islands were home to the Minoans. They constructed large, sophisticated palaces that tripled as royal residences, food-distribution depots, and religious centers. The Minoans also conducted vigorous trade relations with foreign peoples as distant as Egypt.

On the other hand, Greece's mainland was the domain of the Mycenaeans, who spoke an early form of Greek. They erected several massive stone palaces, each of which stood at the center of a small independent kingdom. The one that grew up around Athens was destined to develop over time into one of classical Greece's leading city-states.

Archaeological evidence shows that around 1400 BCE the Mycenaeans attacked and seized control of the Minoan population centers, as well as the islanders' lucrative trade routes. During the two centuries that followed, the mainlanders dominated the region. At some point between 1200 and 1150 BCE, however, the entire Mycenaean-Minoan civilization rapidly declined and broke down. Exactly why this occurred remains unclear. Historians have proposed a number of theories to explain it, ranging from financial ruin to an invasion of peoples native to the region north of Greece.

A Highly Romanticized Lost World

In whatever manner Greece's Bronze Age civilization collapsed, the residents of the Greek lands now slipped into a cultural dark age. Because the palace-centers on the mainland and nearby islands were no longer regularly inhabited and maintained, they swiftly deteriorated. Meanwhile, the arts, literacy, record keeping, and other facets of civilized life faded and, in many areas, disappeared. Overall, says former University of Louisville scholar Robert B. Kebric, "the quality of life declined for most Greeks."[7] With scattered, rare exceptions, they largely reverted to a village-centered and impoverished society.

mneme

The Greek word for *memory*

Moreover, the *mneme*, or memory, of the vanished civilization steadily faded as well, and in general people forgot their own heritage. Recollections of important leaders and events gave way, Kebric explains, to "a tangled collection of orally transmitted stories that had been corrupted [and] embellished over the centuries." And as more and more time elapsed, those fragmentary glimpses of the past grew increasingly hazy and inclined toward exaggeration. They also mixed with a few fables that were either borrowed from nearby foreign lands or simply made up. In this way, the world described in those tales became distorted; it morphed into visions of a society and era that never actually existed. That remote age, Kebric states, became as far removed to the classical Greeks "as the Columbus story is to us today."[8]

Furthermore, the highly romanticized world described in the myths was extremely compelling to the classical Greeks. As C.M. Bowra put it, they "cherished legends of that resplendent past." With the sense of yearning and reverence that people tend to

> feel for a greatness which they cannot recover or rival, the Greeks saw in this lost society something heroic and superhuman, which embodied an ideal of what men should be and do and suffer. Their imaginations, inflamed by ancient stories of vast undertakings and incomparable heroes, of gods walking on the earth as friends of men [formed] a vision of a heroic world which they cherished as one of their most precious possessions.[9]

The Most Celebrated Myths

Probably the most cherished, or at least the most celebrated, of all the Greek myths were those associated with Homer. In the centuries following the Dark Age (ca. 1150–ca. 800 BCE), numerous storytellers, known as bards, roamed the Greek sphere. Homer, who is thought to have flourished in the 700s BCE, became the most famous and beloved of them. He and the others collected and publicly recited the various myths, including the two longest and most popular ones. They recounted the legendary events of the Trojan War and the later wanderings of one of its main participants—the hero Odysseus.

These stories reached their pinnacle of literary quality in Homer's versions, embodied in two magnificent epic poems. The first, the *Iliad*, describes the last year of the Greeks' decade-long siege of Troy; it culminates in a riveting fight to the death between the Greek warrior Achilles and the Trojan champion Hector. The other

As shocked residents of Troy watch from atop their battlements, the Greek warrior Achilles drags the lifeless body of the Trojan champion Hector after defeating him in deadly single combat.

Homeric epic, the *Odyssey*, tells how, after helping defeat the Trojans, Odysseus and his soldiers got lost at sea and endured ten years of danger-filled adventures. Today universally acclaimed as among the finest examples of world literature, the Homeric poems were in a very real sense the national epics of all the classical Greek city-states and kingdoms. The late historian Michael Grant said that the two works "supplied the Greeks with their greatest civilizing influence, and formed the foundation of their literary, artistic, moral, social, educational, and political attitudes. . . . They attracted universal esteem and reverence, too, as sources of general and practical wisdom, as arguments for heroic yet human nobility and dignity . . . and as mines of endless quotations and commentaries."[10]

Recording the Myths for Posterity

Another important contribution Homer made to the myths the classical Greeks revered was to provide fairly detailed depictions of the gods inhabiting those stories. Another early Greek epic poet, Hesiod (a younger contemporary of Homer), did the same. Later, in the fifth century BCE, the well-known Greek historian Herodotus remarked, "It was only, if I may so put it, the day before yesterday that the Greeks came to know the origin and form of the various gods, and whether or not all of them had always existed; for Homer and Hesiod are the poets who described the gods for us, giving them all their appropriate titles, offices, and powers."[11]

Hesiod also collected most of the Greek creation stories in his epic, the *Theogony* (literally, "The Lineage of the Gods"). Among the other major Greek writers who recorded the diverse myths for posterity were the playwrights Aeschylus, Sophocles, and Euripides and the poets Pindar and Apollonius of Rhodes.

As it turned out, the ancient Greeks were not the only ones who benefited from the bards, poets, and other writers who initially wrote down the myths. The characters and events of those tales are so inspiring and appealing that they easily outlived the classical Greeks. And today, well over two thousand years later, they are no less popular in cultures around the globe. Grant pointed out that whether people read the myths, hear them recited, or see them portrayed on film, they are regularly transported to colorful, captivating places and times that stir the imagination. The Greek mythical gods and heroes "carry us with them in their struggles and sufferings," he wrote. And when they fight for justice or overcome monsters or evildoers, "so do we."[12]

CHAPTER TWO

Foremost Gods and Goddesses

One of the most essential aspects of Greek mythology consists of the personalities and tales of the gods, called *theoi* in Greek. These supernatural beings play roles, some big, others small, in nearly all the myths, and those stories were fundamental aspects of ancient Greek religion. Thought by the Greeks to be semi-historical, they were somewhat equivalent to the tales in the biblical Old Testament, a key work underlying the Judeo-Christian religious system.

theoi

The Greek word for the gods

Beyond religion, however, the Greek gods and their stories were, and remain, powerful and appealing as universal comments on the human condition. Those stories have been relatable to people in all ages in part because the Greeks envisioned the beings making up the pantheon, or entire group of gods, as having human qualities. This made the gods appear more understandable and accessible to people of all walks of life. In addition, those super-beings dwelled in a fantastic, fabled world filled with mystical and marvelous phenomena and heroic exploits. As a result, the myths containing the gods never cease to entertain.

Aphrodite

One of the Olympians, she was the goddess of love and beauty, and her chief symbols were doves, dolphins, and roses. The early Greek epic poet Hesiod claimed she first arose from a mass of sea foam, an image that numerous artists have captured over the centuries. In an alternative myth, Aphrodite was a daughter Zeus, leader of the gods, and a minor nature goddess.

The Trojan prince Paris chooses Aphrodite, goddess of love, as the most beautiful of the female Olympians, while two other competing goddesses, Athena and Hera, look on in jealousy and disappointment.

pantheon

A group of gods worshipped
by a people; contains the
Greek word *pan*, meaning *all*,
in this case "all the gods"

The love goddess married Hephaestos, the blacksmith of Mount Olympus. But she had a secret affair with the war god Ares, with whom she had a son— Eros, later her frequent companion. Aphrodite's most famous myth involved an event known as the Judgment of Paris. In it, a prince of Troy named Paris was selected to judge which goddess was the most beautiful. He chose Aphrodite, and in gratitude she thereafter aided him against his enemies.

Apollo

An incredibly versatile deity, he not only could prophecy future events but also oversaw music, healing, poetry, and archery. Apollo, whose main symbol was the laurel tree, was an offspring of Zeus and the goddess Leto and was the twin brother of the goddess of hunting, Artemis. Apollo is renowned for his oracle (temple where he delivered prophecies) at Delphi, in central Greece, visited by ancient religious pilgrims from across the known world.

Among the many myths in which the god appears, one of the most dramatic is the one in which he and his sister achieved revenge on a Theban woman named Niobe, who had insulted their divine mother. The twin deities punished the woman by attacking her seven sons and seven daughters. After slaying the seven boys, the enraged Apollo and his sister turned on the seven girls. According to the ancient myth teller Ovid, "The twang of the [divine] bowstrings rang out, bringing terror."[13] Soon, all fourteen of Niobe's offspring lay dead before her horrified eyes.

Ares

The god of war, Ares had the distinction of being the only child born of the marriage between Zeus and Hera, "queen" of the gods. Conceited and prone to violent outbursts, Ares was often portrayed in art carrying his symbols—a spear and a burning torch. From his affair with the love goddess Aphrodite, he gained twin sons—Deimos and Phobos—who sometimes fought alongside him in battle.

Indeed, Ares was best known for his exploits on the battlefield, where he displayed true bravery and fighting skill. Counteracting those positive traits, however, he was not very bright, which allowed other gods to sometimes outwit or humiliate him. In one famous story, for example, during the siege of Troy the war goddess Athena helped a Greek soldier wound Ares. The latter retaliated by throwing his spear at Athena. But it bounced off her armor, leaving her untouched. She then hurled a large rock, knocking him to ground, and laughed at him.

Artemis

The goddess of wild animals, hunting, and archery and Apollo's twin sister, she had deer, dogs, and cypress trees as symbols. Artemis was a virgin and quite proud of it; often she urged other female deities to refrain from sex. In most of her myths, she was a strong, no-nonsense character. For instance, when a man named Actaeon glimpsed Artemis bathing naked, she angrily transformed him into a deer. Actaeon's own dogs then killed him.

Athena

Goddess of war and *sophia*, or wisdom, Athena was not born normally, but instead burst out of Zeus's head clad in full armor. Her principal symbols were the owl and olive tree. In fact, she gave Athens its first olive tree, thereby defeating her brother Poseidon in a contest to see which would become that city's patron deity. Subsequently, in the role of Athens's divine protector, she was often called Athena Polias, or "Athena of the City."

In one of her best-known myths, Athena addressed the plight of Orestes, son of the Greek

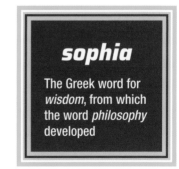

sophia

The Greek word for *wisdom*, from which the word *philosophy* developed

king Agamemnon. Driven by a family curse inflicted by the gods, Orestes had slain his own mother. He then fled to Athens and there fell on Athena's mercy. After considering all available evidence, she decided to forgive his sin of matricide and lifted the curse as well.

Demeter

The Greek goddess of plants, particularly grain crops, her main symbol was a sheaf of wheat. In her chief myth, her brother, Hades, ruler of the underworld, kidnapped her daughter, Persephone, and took her to his dark realm. Not realizing what had happened, Demeter left Mount Olympus and frantically searched for her daughter. Zeus begged for Demeter to return. But as one ancient document said, "She declared she would not set foot on sweet-smelling Olympus . . . before she looked upon her fair daughter again."[14] Eventually, mother and daughter were reunited for half of each year. (Persephone had to spend the other half in the underworld as Hades's mate.)

Dionysus

The deity of fertility, the vine, and wine, he was a son of Zeus and the youngest of the leading gods. The best-known of Dionysus's myths was dramatized in Euripides's play the *Bacchae*. The god drove the city's women into a mindless frenzy, causing them to dance relentlessly while wandering through the countryside. The Theban king, Pentheus, retaliated by jailing the young god. But that turned out to be a mistake. Dionysus persuaded the ruler to disguise himself as a female and go join the dancing women. When Pentheus did so, those women, still in a trance, saw the king as a wild animal and tore him apart.

Hades

He was overseer of the underworld, and his primary symbol was the scepter, or staff, that signified his power as a ruler. Although he was a grim, unemotional character who punished evildoers,

Hades was not himself evil or unjust. Thus, he is not viewed as the equivalent of the Christian Devil. Nevertheless, he was widely feared, and saying his name was thought to be unlucky. Perhaps for those reasons, Hades appeared in very few myths. The best known was the one in which he abducted Persephone, daughter of the goddess Demeter. He made the young woman queen of his kingdom, where she lived during half of each year. (She spent the other half with her mother on earth's surface.)

Hephaestos

Blacksmith of the Olympian gods and patron of craftspeople, he was the son of Zeus and Hera in some myths and the child of Hera by herself in others. His symbols were an anvil and hammer. One of his key myths claimed that Hera hated that the infant Hephaestos had a lame leg, so she tossed him off Mount Olympus into the sea. Fortunately, the sea deity Thetis found him and secretly raised him in a cave. According to historians Michael Grant and John Hazel, "It was there he learned his [blacksmith's] arts. He fashioned a golden throne for his mother and sent it to her; but he had concealed in it a trap. . . . When she sat on the throne she was imprisoned."[15] Only Hephaestos could free her, which he did after becoming Mount Olympus's blacksmith.

Hera

A sister and later the wife of Zeus, she was queen of the Olympian gods and a major protector of marriage and women's life. Her symbols were the pomegranate and peacock. Her best-known myths are those in which she repeatedly became jealous over Zeus's affairs with goddesses and mortals alike and retaliated against his lovers. One of them was Alcmena, mother of the famous strongman Heracles. Zeus impregnated Alcmena, and Hera tried but failed to get revenge by causing Heracles to be stillborn.

Poseidon

Often brandishing his main symbol—a three-pronged spear, or trident—he was the primary god of seas and other waterways and Zeus's brother. Poseidon was called the "earth shaker" because it was thought that he caused earthquakes. Of the numerous myths in which he appeared, an important one was connected to the Trojan War and its aftermath. Poseidon disliked the Trojans and often obstructed them during the Greeks' siege of Troy. At war's end, however, at the request of his divine niece, Athena, he punished some of the Greeks by generating a storm that swamped their ships. One of the Greek leaders, Odysseus, survived. But soon afterward Odysseus blinded Poseidon's son, the Cyclops Polyphemus, thereby initiating the sea god's long-lasting hostility.

Zeus

In addition to being the ruler of the gods, he held sway in a number of important areas. They included controlling thunder, lightning, and rain; maintaining justice and morality; and overseeing the laws of hospitality and punishing those who broke them. His main symbols were the thunderbolt, eagle, and oak tree. Greeks everywhere erected temples and other shrines to him, the most renowned being the Temple of Olympian Zeus at Olympia—site of the ancient Olympic Games—in southwestern Greece.

Considering his great stature, it is not surprising that Zeus appeared in dozens of myths. One of the most important involved his birth and those of his divine siblings. In his *Theogony*, the early Greek poet Hesiod said Zeus was the youngest of the six offspring of Cronos and Rhea, members of the first race of gods, the Titans. The crude Cronos worried that one of his children might try to destroy him. So he swallowed each at birth. In this way, Poseidon, Hera, Hades, Hestia, and Demeter all ended up in his enormous stomach. The ordeal did not kill them because they were divine and therefore immortal.

Zeus, leader of the Olympian gods, hurls a thunderbolt (streak of lightning) at one of his enemies. Because of his ability to control that natural force, the thunderbolt became one of his personal symbols.

Rhea was very upset over losing her babies. So when the sixth one—Zeus—came along, she substituted a big stone for the infant, and Cronos, who was too dim-witted to notice, swallowed it. Raised in secret in a faraway place, Zeus grew to adulthood and set out to save his siblings. He forced Cronos to vomit them up, and they became the nucleus of a new race of gods— the Olympians.

CHAPTER THREE

Nature Deities and Other Minor Gods

A large number of the tales in the Greek mythological corpus deal in one way or another with nature. In the words of Stanford University scholar Adrienne Mayor, "Greek myth is a complex skein [knotted thread] of tales about the origin of the natural world and the history of its inhabitants."[16] Some of those stories explain in fanciful ways how the moon, planets, and other heavenly bodies came to be. Other myths involve weather phenomena, such as thunder and lightning, or natural disasters like earthquakes.

The classical Greeks believed that these and the world's other natural elements were controlled by various gods. A few of those deities, like Poseidon, who generated earthquakes, were among the most powerful. But a majority of them were minor gods. Not all the lesser divinities were connected to natural phenomena. Some had other essential duties, such as overseeing childbirth, bringing victory in battle, and providing inspiration for poets and artists.

Whatever their functions, the Greek gods, even the minor ones, were both physically familiar and quite comprehensible to people because they had human form. As the late, great modern mythologist Edith Hamilton said, those

beings "were exceedingly and humanly attractive." That is "the miracle of Greek mythology," she pointed out, "a humanized world [in which people were] freed from the paralyzing fear of . . . unknown [forces]."[17]

Asclepius

The Greek god of healing, he was the son of the god of prophecy, Apollo. Asclepius was said to have married a mortal woman who bore him two sons—Machaon and Podalirius. Also healers, they supposedly helped wounded soldiers during the Trojan War.

The chief ancient tale about Asclepius describes his death, an uncommon end for a divine being. Besides healing the sick, he sometimes dabbled in the dark art of trying to bring dead people back to life. That angered Zeus, who saw such activities as immoral. As a punishment, the ruler of the gods heaved a white-hot thunderbolt at Asclepius, killing him instantly.

Eileithyia

The goddess of childbirth; the early Greek poet Hesiod said she was a daughter of Zeus and Hera. This may be why Eileithyia often did Hera's bidding. In the chief myth in which Eileithyia appears, Hera was jealous of Alcmena, mother of the hero Heracles. When Alcmena was in labor with him, Hera ordered Eileithyia to sit nearby with her arms, legs, fingers, and toes crossed. This was meant to place a hex on the birth and thereby cause the baby to be stillborn. The plan failed, however, when Eileithyia became distracted and uncrossed her appendages. To Hera's dismay, Heracles made it safely into the world.

Eros

The god of love and sexual fertility; the Greeks had two separate traditions for his origins. In one, first described by the poet Hesiod, Eros was among the first divine beings to emerge from Chaos—the swirling mass of matter that existed at the universe's

inception. Supposedly, he brought light to a dark cosmos and caused Gaia (the earth) and Uranus (the sky) to mate and produce the first race of gods, the Titans. In the second main myth about Eros, he was born the son of the love goddess Aphrodite and war god Ares. Exceedingly attractive and athletic, Eros was often depicted by Greek artists carrying his chief symbol—a bow and arrow.

Gaia

A conscious, divine spirit, the earth itself was her body, and many Greeks called her Mother Earth. According to Hesiod in his *Theogony*, shortly after the world emerged from Chaos, Gaia mated with the sky, Uranus, and that union produced a large number of children. In addition to the Titans, the first race of gods, those offspring included many misshapen, monstrous beings. Among them were the "unspeakable Kottos and Gyes and Briareus, insolent children, each with a hundred [hands],"[18] Hesiod said, and three huge one-eyed giants called Cyclopes.

Helios

The sun god, his name is the Greek word for the sun, *helios*. The Greeks pictured him as a stalwart father figure who drove a blindingly bright chariot across the sky each day. His principal myth involved the tragedy of his young son, Phaethon, who had come from the union of the god and a mortal woman. The boy requested that he be allowed to drive the gleaming chariot. At first, Helios said no because it would be too dangerous. But Phaethon insisted, and his father eventually relented. The trouble began when the horses sensed that a stranger was piloting the vehicle, and according to the ancient myth teller

helios

The Greek word for the sun, from which came the name of the sun god, Helios, and the modern word *heliocentric*, or sun-centered

Ovid, they "ran wild and left the well-worn highway." The young driver soon lost control, and the horses "ran amok amid the stars fixed in the vault of heaven, hurtling the chariot where no road had run."[19] As the chariot crashed to earth, large forests burst into flame, and Phaethon met a fiery death, leaving Helios grief-stricken.

Hermes

The gods' messenger, he was also the divine patron of travelers and merchants. His chief symbol was a herald's staff, and artists often depicted him wearing winged sandals and a winged hat. In one of his main myths, he accompanied Zeus on a journey through a Greek valley. Disguised as mortal beggars, the two divinities tested the locals by going door-to-door and asking for aid. They were repeatedly turned away. Finally, they came to the home of the dirt-poor Baucis and Philemon, who invited them in and shared with them what little food they had. Impressed by that show of hospitality, Hermes and Zeus spared the aged couple when the two gods flooded the valley to punish its other residents.

Iris

The goddess of rainbows, she also carried messages for Hera and other deities. Though physically beautiful, Iris was sister to the hideous flying creatures called Harpies, and in her main myth she protected them. Some of the hero Jason's men—the Argonauts—were about to slay the Harpies for trying to starve an old man named Phineus. But Iris intervened. She made a deal with the men, promising that if they spared her sisters, she would keep the Harpies away from Phineus. The bargain was kept by all involved.

Muses

Nine of Zeus's numerous daughters, they were thought to provide inspiration for poets, musicians, painters, and writers. The early Greek epic poet Hesiod credited them with making him an effective storyteller and mentioned them in the opening of his *Theogony*, saying, "Hail, daughters of Zeus! Give me sweet song, to celebrate the holy race of gods who live forever. . . . Tell how the gods and earth arose at first, and rivers and the boundless swollen sea and shining stars, and the broad heaven above."[20]

Nike

The winged goddess of victory, she was said to be the daughter of Pallas, the Titan war god. During the Persian Wars (490–479 BCE), the Greeks believed that she helped them defeat the invading Persians in a series of epic battles. To commemorate her aid, in the 430s BCE the Athenian sculptor Phidias fashioned a 6-foot-tall (1.8 m) figure of her. It stood upright in the open palm of his enormous statue of the war goddess, Athena, inside the newly erected Parthenon temple.

Nymphs

The Greeks believed that these minor female nature deities were almost countless in number. Supposedly, they helped maintain earth's and heaven's uncorrupted beauty; made trees, flowers, and other plants grow; and preserved the integrity of mountains, beaches, forests, caves, and other natural settings. Each setting tended to have a group of nymphs. For example, the Dryads maintained trees; the Oreads mountains; the Naiads lakes, rivers, and springs; and the Epimelides grassy pastures and orchards. Among the most famous individual nymphs was Echo. Deciding she was too talkative, Zeus's wife, Hera, limited her speaking to repeating the last word she heard someone say, which explains the derivation of the word *echo*.

Pan

Son of the messenger god Hermes, Pan was the deity of shepherds, pastures, and flocks. Greek artists most often depicted Pan with a human upper body and the lower body of a goat. He frequently brandished an flute-like instrument, the "panpipe,"

which he himself invented. In one of his primary myths, he employed a distinct physical gift—an incredibly loud, at times frightening voice. While aiding Zeus's forces in a major battle against an army of giants, Pan yelled at the enemy, many of whom panicked and ran for their lives.

Prometheus

One of the Titans, the first race of gods, he was known as the deity of foresight because of his wisdom and good judgment. The classical Greeks came to see him as humanity's savior, based on his main myth. In that famous story, Zeus requested that he create a race of mortals called *anthropoi*, or human beings. Prometheus shaped their bodies from river mud. These "creatures of Prometheus," as Zeus called them, lacked fire, so they were often cold, hungry, and miserable. Although Zeus forbade the gods from giving them fire, Prometheus took pity on them. He stole some fire from Mount Olympus and gifted it to his creations, thereby saving humanity. Zeus was so angry, he ordered that Prometheus be chained to a mountaintop, where he was daily tortured by a giant vulture (or eagle, in some accounts).

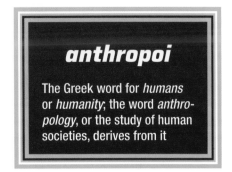

anthropoi

The Greek word for *humans* or *humanity*; the word *anthropology*, or the study of human societies, derives from it

Thanatos

The Greeks saw him as the deity of death, a sort of grim reaper who came to claim people's shades, or souls, after they died. Usually, he performed that duty without incident. But on occasion a human outsmarted or otherwise evaded him. A gripping example is the subject of his best-known myth. As dramatized in Euripides's great play *Alcestis*, the title character agreed to die in place of her beloved husband, Admetus. Accordingly, Thanatos, clad in a black robe, arrived to take her soul. Luckily for her, however, the hero Heracles had planned to rescue her by ambushing the deity. "Once I have my arms locked round his bruised ribs," the strongman exclaimed (in Euripides's words), "there's no power on earth that will be able to wrench him free, till he gives her up to me!"[21] In a fantastic wrestling bout, Heracles proceeded to defeat Thanatos, forcing him to retreat without his prize.

Titans

Called the *titanes* in Greek, they were the deities making up the first race of gods. The offspring of the early divine forces Gaia

(earth) and Uranus (sky), they were very large, powerful beings having human form. Their leader was Cronos, father of Zeus, Poseidon, and other beings who later became the Olympian gods. Other important Titans included Rhea (Cronos's mate and goddess of fertility), Oceanus (god of seas and rivers), Hyperion (god of light), Phoebe (goddess of prophecy), and Iapetus (god of life and death). Perhaps the most crucial myth in which the Titans appeared was that of the Titanomachia—a massive battle for the universe, pitting the Titans against Zeus and his Olympians. After ten years of ceaseless fighting that decimated earth's surface, the Olympians won and imprisoned the surviving Titans in Tartarus, the underworld's deepest, gloomiest sector.

CHAPTER FOUR

Renowned Human Heroes

Of the many compelling tales in their grand corpus of myths, the classical Greeks were especially drawn to those featuring heroes. Seen as *aristos*, or "best," among humans, some of those larger-than-life characters possessed almost superhuman bravery and fighting skills. They stood out in pivotal battles and slew terrifying monsters or corrupt rulers. Other heroes earned renown by exhibiting great selflessness, an uncommon sense of morality and justice, or a noble spirit.

aristos

A Greek word meaning *best*, from which the word *aristocrat* comes; heroes like Heracles were seen as best among humans

Endowed with such qualities, the mythical heroes set examples for ordinary Greeks to emulate. It is not surprising, therefore, that those stalwart individuals occupied a special position in Greek culture and its traditions. They lacked the divine stature of the gods, the late historian W.H.D. Rouse pointed out. The heroes of old, he wrote, "were not immortal. Their bodies died." Yet both the gods and ordinary humans saw them as deserving of the highest praise and privilege. As a result, following their deaths, Rouse says, the heroes "were worshiped on earth and their souls lived still, and some went to the Isles of the Blessed,"[22] a sector of the underworld that was free from worry and strife.

Achilles

One of the leading Greek warriors who fought in the Trojan War, he was also the main character in the *Iliad*, Homer's epic poem describing that conflict. Achilles was the son of the sea deity Thetis and a Greek ruler named Peleus. Thetis lowered her infant son's body into the Styx, the river bordering the underworld. That caused him to become resistant to physical harm, except in the heel by which she held him. Achilles's most familiar myth is the one in which he fought the Trojan prince Hector. The latter had slain Achilles's friend Patroclus, and to obtain revenge, Achilles clashed with Hector before Troy's towering walls. Although victorious, Achilles was himself doomed. Another Trojan prince, Paris, shot a poisoned arrow into his heel—his one vulnerable spot—thereby killing him.

Alcestis

One of the few female heroes in Greek mythology, she was the daughter of Pelias, king of the Greek kingdom of Iolcos. Her legendary valor stems from the extraordinary love, loyalty, and courage she displayed by offering to die in place of her ailing husband, Admetus. Fortunately for her, as Euripides told it in his play *Alcestis*, the muscular hero Heracles arrived just in time to prevent the god of death, Thanatos, from claiming her soul. As a result, she and Admetus had many more happy years together.

Antigone

A female tragic hero, she was a daughter of Oedipus, king of Thebes. After her brothers, Polynices and Eteocles, drove their father from the city and seized the throne, Eteocles turned on Polynices, who retaliated by attacking Thebes. Subsequently, as told in Sophocles's great play *Oedipus at Colonus*, the brothers clashed and killed each other. Then the new king, their uncle Creon, committed an act the Greeks viewed as monstrous; he denied Polynices a decent burial. At this, Antigone daringly defied the ruler's edict and buried her brother, after which the furious Creon ordered her execution. To the Greeks, her insistence on doing the right thing, knowing she would die for it, was an example of heroism of the highest order.

Bellerophon

Son of Glaucus, king of Corinth, Bellerophon was one of Greek mythology's premier monster slayers. Iobates, king of the Greek kingdom of Lycia, sent the young man on a mission that most people, including Iobates, were sure would end in his death. A repulsive and frightening creature—the Chimaera—had recently been creating a path of destruction though Lycia's heartland, and it had eaten every warrior sent to stop it. In contrast, Bellerophon was not only brave but also smart. Instead of attacking the monster on foot, he tamed the legendary flying horse, Pegasus, and by riding that magical steed, he outmaneuvered and slaughtered the Chimaera.

Hector

The eldest son of Priam, king of Troy, he was the greatest Trojan warrior during the Greeks' famous siege of the city. As described by Homer in his *Iliad*, Hector fought and slew numerous Greeks during the war. But the Trojan prince's most memorable fight was the one against the Greeks' leading warrior—Achilles. The two champions met in single combat as the respective armies looked on. Drawing his sword, Homer said, Hector "swooped like a soaring eagle" at Achilles, who "charged too, bursting with rage." After an incredible display of fighting skills by both men, Achilles saw an opening and drove his spear into Hector's neck. That proved the death blow. As Homer described it, "The end closed in around" valiant Hector. "Flying free of his limbs, his soul went winging down to the House of Death, leaving his manhood far behind."[23]

Heracles

Better known in later ages, including today, by his Roman name, Hercules, he was arguably the greatest Greek mythical hero of all. He was certainly the strongest of the heroes and fought and killed more monsters and other dangerous creatures than any of the others. Moreover, the question of whether he would win was never in doubt. As Edith Hamilton put it, "Whenever he fought with anyone, the issue was certain beforehand. He could be overcome only by a supernatural force."[24]

This modern painting depicts the mighty hero Heracles wrestling a lion. According to various ancient accounts, the strongman squeezed the life out of the beast and then wore its pelt.

One of Heracles's earliest opponents was also one of the most memorable. It was an enormous lion that was killing sheep, goats, and people on the slopes of Mount Cithaeron, near Thebes. Hearing about this menace, Heracles, still a teenager, tracked down the beast, wrestled it to the ground, and slapped a crushing bear hug on it. One after another, the lion's bones crackled and snapped until all life drained from its body. Wasting no time, Heracles skinned the creature and thereafter wore its hide over his tunic.

Jason and the Argonauts

Son of Aeson, a former king of Iolcos, in central Greece, Jason was best known for leading one of the greatest heroic quests in all of world mythology. The tyrant Pelias, who had usurped the throne from Aeson, challenged Jason to find the Golden Fleece, the hide of a famous, magical ram. To that end, Jason acquired a sturdy ship—the *Argo*—and gathered together a crew of skilled sailors and fighters—the so-called Argonauts. Among them were the mighty hero Heracles; Zetes and Calais, the winged sons of a wind god; and in some ancient accounts the fearless female hunter and warrior Atalanta.

As told by Apollonius of Rhodes in his epic, the *Argonautica*, the heroes sailed out of the Aegean Sea and into the Black Sea. After several hair-raising adventures, they reached their destination—the land of Colchis, where the local king, Aeetes, guarded the Golden Fleece. In his most dangerous adventure yet, Jason had to fight an army of warriors that grew from special seeds Aeetes had planted. In a fantastic display of courage—aided by magic wielded by Aeetes's daughter, Medea, who had fallen in love with Jason—the hero defeated the seed warriors. Then the chief Argonaut swiped the Golden Fleece and, with Medea at his side, took it back to Greece.

Odysseus

Ruler of the Greek island kingdom of Ithaca, he was one of the main leaders of the Greek siege of Troy. He is also the principal character of Homer's immortal epic poem the *Odyssey*, meaning a long arduous journey, a word derived from his name. Odysseus's most famous contribution to mythology began shortly after Troy's fall to the Greeks. A massive storm conjured up by the sea god Poseidon blew his twelve ships off course, and he ended up wandering through strange regions for ten years.

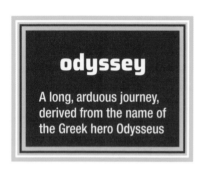

Among the many adventures that occurred on that journey, one of the scariest occurred when Odysseus and a handful of his soldiers searched for food on an island inhabited by a race of giant one-eyed creatures—the Cyclopes. One of those ogres—Polyphemus by name—trapped the men in his cave and killed and ate several of them before the others blinded him. While he roared in rage and stumbled around, they made it back to the ships. But later, Odysseus discovered that Polyphemus was Poseidon's son, and thereafter that god frequently sought vengeance by striking out at Odysseus and his followers. When the Ithacan king finally made it home after ten years of war and ten years of wandering, all of his ships had been destroyed and all of his men had died.

Perseus

A son of Zeus and a mortal woman named Danae, his heroic reputation derived from his slaying of perhaps the most notorious monster in all of Greek mythology—Medusa. She was said to have snakes for hair, and supposedly the sight of her was so frightening that it turned both humans and animals to stone. Perseus realized that he was at a disadvantage. He did not know the location of the remote island where Medusa lived. Also, he needed a way to avoid being turned to stone. Fortunately, he received divine aid. The messenger god Hermes told him the location of the island and gave him winged sandals that allowed him to fly. Hermes also gifted him a special cap that

Athena, goddess of war and wisdom, presents Perseus with a special shield. Its surface was so highly polished that he was able to view the monstrous Medusa via reflection and thereby avoid being turned to stone.

rendered him invisible. The war goddess Athena gave Perseus a polished shield in which he could view Medusa's harmless reflection.

With these advantages, the young man flew through the *aer*, or atmosphere, to the island and there beheld a disturbing sight. In the ancient myth teller Ovid's words, "No matter where he turned he saw both man and beast turned into stone, all creatures who had seen Medusa's face."[25] Not long afterward,

Perseus found Medusa sunning herself on big rock overlooking the sea. Careful to glance only at her reflection in the shield, he swooped down and swung his sword, neatly separating her ghastly head from her no less unsightly body.

Theseus

Son of Aegeus, king of Athens during the Age of Heroes, Theseus was the classical Athenians' national father figure. In addition to his many heroic exploits, Theseus supposedly brought together the scattered villages of the Attic Peninsula into the Athenian nation-state. His most famous myth was the one in which he saved fourteen young Athenians who had been taken hostage by Minos, the tyrant king of the large Greek island of Crete. There they were to be fed to the Minotaur, a ravenous monster that was half bull and half human. Descending into the Labyrinth, the maze of dungeons lying beneath Minos's palace, Theseus found the creature and used his sword to dispatch it. Then the young hero freed the hostages and brought them home to Athens.

CHAPTER FIVE

Monsters and Other Mythical Beasts

It would not be an overstatement to say that the classical Greeks were infatuated with myths about monstrous creatures. Actually, stories about *zoia*, or animals, in general fascinated them. This can be seen by the fact that their myths abound with horses, wild boars, dogs, and lions, as well as human-animal hybrids such as the half-human and half-goat creatures known as satyrs.

The monsters were therefore only the most extreme of the huge array of beasts that populated the Age of Heroes—the fantastic past era the classical Greeks looked back on with such admiration. Modern experts think this fascination for natural beasts, especially the dangerous, scary kind, reflected the dual character of ancient Greek society. That fascination for the wild and grotesque in a sense balanced the Greeks' equally strong love of order, harmony, and artistic beauty. In their view, order had evolved from *dis*order, and one could not appreciate

zoia

The Greek word for *animals*, from which the modern word *zoo* derives

beauty and goodness without recognizing the existence of ugliness and evil.

Thus, states University of Oxford scholar Peter Stewart, Greek civilization possessed two contrasting images. There was a sort of "distorting mirror in which the Greeks could look at themselves." They saw the "monstrous or semi-human creatures useful to explore and express their world-view, their ideas about humanity and civilization, the mortal and divine. Fantastical beings were part of the furniture of the Greek mind."[26]

Argus

He was Odysseus's faithful dog in the complex story told in Homer's *Odyssey*. When the Ithacan king departed for Troy, he left behind Argus, then a puppy. Twenty years later, the hero returned, and in one of the most poignant scenes in Western literature, the aged and ailing Argus joyfully recognizes his master. "He wagged his tail and dropped his ears," Homer wrote. Drinking in the gratifying sight, "after twenty years of waiting, he looked upon his beloved master." Then faithful Argus leisurely shut his eyes "as death's dark hand closed over him."[27]

Centaurs

Said to be the offspring of the god Apollo, centaurs were creatures having the upper bodies of humans and the lower bodies of horses. According to legend, most centaurs were untidy, uneducated, crude characters. The notable exception was Chiron, a polite, well-educated individual who served as personal tutor to several well-known Greek heroes.

The best-known myth featuring the centaurs tells how they fought a war with an early group of Greeks called the Lapiths. Pirithous, ruler of the Lapiths, invited several centaurs to his wedding. He regretted it, for the horse-men got drunk and aggressive and ran off with some Lapith women. Several Lapith warriors gave chase and in a bloody fight slew numerous centaurs. The classical Greeks called that mythical battle the Centauromachy.

Cerberus, an enormous and vicious three-headed dog, guarded the entrance to the underworld. As one of his trials, or labors, Heracles (shown) was to capture Cerberus and bring him to the Greek king Eurystheus.

Cerberus

The enormous three-headed dog that guarded the entrance to the underworld, the vicious Cerberus seized and devoured any human souls that attempted to escape their fates in Hades's dark realm. The beast also attacked any living people who tried to enter the underworld. That is why the poet and musician Orpheus, bent on rescuing his lover, Eurydice, played music when near the creature; hearing it, Cerberus grew calm, and the man was able to slip by. In one of the giant dog's most famous myths, at the command of a Greek king named Eurystheus, the renowned strongman Heracles captured it. After the king and his subjects beheld the creature with a mix of awe and fear, Eurystheus ordered Heracles to return it to the underworld, and the hero did so.

Charybdis

A dangerous female monster, she bore the shape of a big, swirling whirlpool. She laid in wait for ships and sailors passing through Sicily's Strait of Messina. The best-known mythical incident involving Charybdis occurred when the hero Odysseus passed through the strait during his decade of wandering. Having by this time lost his ships and men, Odysseus managed to grab hold of the branch of a fig tree that overhung the whirlpool and thereby escaped.

Cyclopes

The Greeks had multiple mythical traditions involving these single-eyed giants. Of the two main ones, the first, described by the early poet Hesiod, said that Gaia (earth) and Uranus (sky) mated and produced three Cyclopes—Arges, Brontes, and Steropes. Fearful of them, Uranus locked them away in the underworld's deepest recesses.

In the second principal tradition, mentioned by Homer in the *Odyssey*, a race of wild, primitive Cyclopes dwelled on a remote island that Odysseus and some of his men explored. The humans were detained in a cave by a Cyclops named Polyphemus, who rolled an enormous rock across the cave opening, trapping them. For two days, one by one the fearsome creature devoured the Greeks, who prayed to Zeus for aid that never came. Finally, Odysseus had the idea to wait till Polyphemus was asleep and drive a red-hot pointed stick through his eye, blinding him. This plan worked, and after the giant removed the rock in order to allow his sheep to graze, the surviving men made their escape. As Homer tells it, the Cyclops shook with a combination of anger and anguish. He then cried out to the sea god Poseidon, requesting that Odysseus "may never reach his home!" Furthermore, "may he lose all his companions, and may he find [troubles] at home!"[28]

Erinyes

These frightening, flying female creatures supposedly sprang from blood droplets that fell to the ground after the Titan Cronos attacked his father, Uranus. Also known as the Furies (their Roman name), they avenged crimes, especially murder, by hunting down a criminal and then harassing and killing him or her. One of the primary myths involving these savage beasts was the one in which they relentlessly pursued a young prince named Orestes after he had killed his mother. Eventually, the goddess Athena intervened and absolved Orestes of his crime. Then she transformed the scary Erinyes into the friendly Eumenides, or "kindly ones."

Giants

Greek mythology contains numerous examples of giants. Among them were Otus and Ephialtes, sons of Poseidon, who grew so fast that when they were only nine they were already 50 feet (15.2 m) tall. Also famous was the hunter Orion. According to legend, he was so tall he could walk on the sea bottom and still keep his head above the water's surface. Perhaps the most renowned giants, however, were those who grew from the blood droplets released when Cronos wounded his father, Uranus. The latter's mate, Gaia, enlisted the aid of these giants when she tried to overthrow Zeus. At her order, the monstrous beings attacked Zeus and his followers, a battle the classical Greeks called the Gigantomachy.

Harpies

Often called "snatchers," they were repulsive-looking, birdlike beasts sporting women's faces. Typically, they appeared seemingly out of nowhere and either stole people's food or covered it with a revolting stink, rendering it inedible. Their chief myth recounted how they harassed a man named Phineus who dwelled on a remote island. When the hero Jason and his crew—the Argonauts—arrived, they vowed to help the old man against the

Harpies. When those creatures next appeared, the Argonauts Zetes and Calais, who could fly, chased after them. The two men were about to slay the Harpies when the creatures' sister, the rainbow deity Iris, intervened. She made a deal whereby the Argonauts agreed to spare the Harpies in exchange for her keeping the food snatchers away from the old man.

Hecatoncheres

The collective name of these three mythical giants means "Hundred-Handers," based on each having one hundred arms, along with fifty heads. Their individual names were Kottus, Briareos, and Gyes, and they were among the many monstrous offspring of the primeval forces Gaia (earth) and Uranus (sky). Afraid that the Hundred-Handers might overpower him, Uranus locked them away in Tartarus, the deepest sector of the underworld. Later, however, Zeus released the three so they could help him defeat the Titans. When that long battle ended, the three giants were assigned the task of guarding the surviving Titans, whom Zeus had imprisoned in Tartarus.

Medusa and the Gorgons

The three Gorgons—Medusa, Stheno, and Euryale by name—were among the most feared monsters in Greek mythology. Early accounts described their appearance variously. Some claimed they were originally beautiful maidens who later grew hideous; others said they were ugly all along. Greek artists most often pictured them with wide grins, protruding tusks, animals' legs, and snakes for hair. It was said that gazing at them caused a person or animal to turn to *lithos*, or stone (although some tales insisted that only Medusa displayed that particular trait). The gorgons dwelled on an uncharted island, and in their most famous myth the hero Perseus journeyed there, slew Medusa, and carried away her head. One ancient account claimed that the healing god Asclepius arrived soon after and scooped up Medusa's remaining blood. "He used it on his patients," Michael Grant and John Hazel explain. Blood from one vein "had the power to revive dead bodies, but the blood coming from another was lethal."[29]

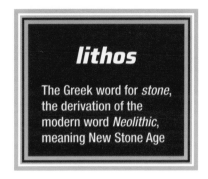

lithos

The Greek word for *stone*, the derivation of the modern word *Neolithic*, meaning New Stone Age

Minotaur

Having the head of a bull and a man's body, this monstrous creature came from the strange coupling of a massive bull and Pasiphae, wife of Minos, king of Crete. When the Minotaur was born, Minos locked it away in the Labyrinth, the maze of dungeons lying under his sprawling palace. There he fed the beast hostages he periodically took from Athens, until the Athenian hero Theseus sailed to Crete, entered the Labyrinth, and cut the bull-man to pieces.

Pegasus

This world-famous flying horse had a singular and strange origin. After the hero Perseus slew the hideous monster Medusa, he noticed something crawling out of her lifeless body. It was the infant Pegasus, conceived long before in a union between the sea god Poseidon and Medusa when she was still physically beautiful. Before the surprised Perseus's eyes, Pegasus flew off into the sky (*polos* in Greek). The magnificent steed remained wild and free until the hero Bellerophon tamed it and then rode it while slaying the monstrous Chimaera.

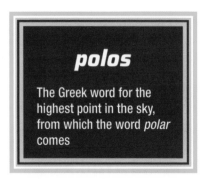

polos

The Greek word for the highest point in the sky, from which the word *polar* comes

Sphinx

According to the ancient writer known today as Pseudo-Apollodorus, this monster "had a woman's face, the breast, feet, and tail of a lion, and birds' wings." She terrorized the Greek city of Thebes, devouring its residents one by one. Before killing them, the creature posed each victim a riddle that went, Pseudo-Apollodorus said, "What [being] has one voice, and is four-footed and two-footed and three-footed?"[30]

No one could answer that question, so the killing continued until a young man named Oedipus arrived in Thebes. He bravely confronted the Sphinx, who posed her usual riddle. She was shocked, however, when Oedipus said the being in the riddle was a human. As an infant it crawls on all fours; later, as an adult, it walks on two feet; and later still, when elderly, it employs a cane, in a sense a third foot. Feeling humiliated, the Sphinx leaped off a towering cliff to her death.

CHAPTER SIX

The Major Ancient Myth Tellers

The modern world would not have inherited the magnificent Greek corpus of myths had it not been for a handful of talented and prolific ancient writers. They committed those tales to paper, allowing them thereafter to pass from one generation to another. The earliest major myth tellers, the epic poets Homer and Hesiod, flourished in the 700s BCE. Their primary contributions were to describe the universe's creation, the gods, and the Trojan War.

Classical Greek writers soon picked up the mantle of myth telling. Huge within their ranks were the great Athenian tragic playwrights—Aeschylus, Sophocles, and Euripides. Their plays can in a very real way be called storehouses of myths. In the words of the late historian Michael Grant, "The subject matter of the Athenian plays dealt with . . . the relationship of mankind with the gods. That is to say, the subjects were mythological."[31]

As time went on, other writers, including the Greek poet Pindar and Roman poet Ovid, also recorded various myths. So did early Greek historians, Herodotus among them. It is extremely fortunate that these and other myth tellers preserved those stories. First, it allowed people in later eras to enjoy the tales themselves. Also, the myths' survival provided the modern world with vital insights into what the ancient Greeks themselves "believed, thought and felt," Grant points out. Their myths were "interwoven, to an extent far beyond anything in our own experience, with the whole fabric of their public and private lives."[32]

Aeschylus

Born in Athens circa 525 BCE, he is often referred to as the world's first true dramatist. Along with Sophocles and Euripides, he was one of the three leading writers of tragedy during Athens's cultural golden age. Aeschylus fought in the pivotal sea battle of Salamis, in which the Greeks defeated the invading Persians, an event he described in his play *The Persians*. The other six of the surviving seven of his estimated eighty plays deal with well-known myths. *The Eumenides*, for example, describes how Athena forgave Orestes for slaying his mother, and *Prometheus Bound* chronicles Zeus's punishment of Prometheus for giving fire to humans.

Apollonius of Rhodes

A Greek poet and scholar born in the early 200s BCE, he served as director of the famous great library at Alexandria (in Egypt) before retiring to the Greek Aegean island of Rhodes. His most renowned work was *Argonautica*, a six-thousand-line epic poem that describes in considerable detail the expedition of Jason and the Argonauts to find the fabulous Golden Fleece. Most modern literary critics view the love affair between Jason and Medea as the work's most powerful section. Apollonius describes Medea as a lovestruck maiden but also as a sorceress and strong, ambitious, capable woman, who is in many ways Jason's equal. That gives their relationship a more modern, compelling dimension, in contrast to the way most ancient writers described female characters—as subservient and largely powerless.

Euripides

One of the three masters of Greek tragedy in the Classic Age, he was born around 485 BCE. Among his chief characteristics as a playwright was his frequent emphasis of ideas and themes that questioned traditional social and religious values. Another hallmark of his work was that his dialogue often revealed what was in a character's psyche—his or her mind or soul. For these reasons, today experts see him as the first dramatist to depict aspects of humanity in a modern way.

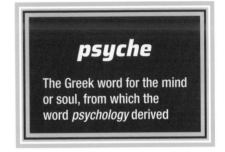

psyche

The Greek word for the mind or soul, from which the word *psychology* derived

Although Euripides likely produced over eighty plays, only nineteen have survived complete. Of those, most deal with mythological characters and events. *Alcestis*, for example, describes the heroism of the title character in offering to die in place of her husband. Several of the playwright's other works also deal with strong mythical women, including *Medea*, *Electra*, and *Helen*.

Herodotus

Considered to be the world's first modern-style historian, he was born in Halicarnassus (in what is now southwestern Turkey) in about 485 BCE. His fame rests on his long work, the *Histories*, which contains a great deal of information about the Greeks and neighboring peoples and nations during his era. That data was not always completely accurate, because he sometimes just repeated rumors he had heard. Nevertheless, thousands of the facts he recorded were largely accurate. His descriptions of the histories of kingdoms and cities at times included local religious beliefs and myths. For example, he traced the origins of some of the stories about the famous heroic strongman Heracles. Herodotus also recorded a more recent myth about Pan, divine protector of shepherds. That deity, he said, approached an Athenian soldier and complained that the Athenians had recently been neglecting him. They "paid him no attention," he explained, "in spite of his friendliness toward them and the fact that he had often been useful to them in the past." Hearing this, Athenian leaders felt bad and "built a shrine to Pan under the Acropolis" and instituted an annual ceremony "with a torch-race and sacrifices, to court his protection."[33]

Hesiod

One of the two great early Greek epic poets (the other being Homer), Hesiod most likely lived in the late 700s and early 600s BCE. He was a farmer in the region of central Greece ruled by Thebes, a fact that he disclosed in his long poem, *Works and Days*. He is most famous for his other epic—*Theogony*, in which he describes most of the early Greek creation myths, including how the universe sprang from a swirling mass of matter called *Khaos* (Chaos). Hesiod also described the early gods—the Titans—and told how they were defeated by the Olympian deities led by "most glorious Zeus, greatest of all the gods who live forever."[34]

Khaos

The Greek word for *Chaos*, the swirling mass of matter that supposedly gave birth to the universe

Homer

Likely flourishing in the early to mid-700s BCE, he was to the classical Greeks far and away the greatest writer of all time. Modern experts think he was one of a series of wandering poets, or bards, who collected myths and both embellished and publicly recited them. The two largest collections of such tales eventually became the *Iliad* and the *Odyssey*. Probably Homer created the final and most literarily impressive versions, which even today are among the most splendid works that Western civilization has ever produced. The noted fourth-century-BCE Athenian thinker Aristotle called Homer "the poet of poets, standing alone not only through [his] literary excellence, but also through the dramatic character of his [works]."[35]

A modern artist here shows Homer reciting verses to passersby. His masterpieces were the final versions of the epic poems the Iliad *and the* Odyssey, *universally seen as two of the greatest literary works of all time.*

Ovid

Born in 43 BCE, Publius Ovidius Naso, called Ovid for short, was not only a gifted Roman poet but also one of the most prolific of all the ancient compilers of the Greek myths. Witty and frequently funny, his poems were also sometimes sexually explicit, which provoked the ire of Rome's first emperor, Augustus. The latter eventually banished Ovid to a small, boring town on the shores of the Black Sea. Fortunately for later generations, the poet left behind the *Metamorphoses*, a beautifully written collection of mythical tales. Mary M. Innes, one of his modern translators, calls it "a treasure-house" and "a source from which the whole of Western European literature has derived inspiration."[36]

Pindar

Born in roughly 518 BCE, he was one of Greece's finest poets. Very little is known about his life, except that he may have been a priest of the god Apollo. Pindar's legacy rests primarily on his "victory odes," longish sets of verses intended to honor the winners of the athletic games held at Olympia and other sites. Several of the odes mention various myths, sometimes offering details not found in other ancient accounts.

Plutarch

Born in about 46 CE, Plutarch was a Greek writer who as an adult became a Roman citizen and lived for a while in the Roman capital. His main claims to fame are two large-scale literary works. One, the *Parallel Lives*, consists of fifty detailed biographies of well-known Greek and Roman rulers, military generals, and other notable figures. The second work is the *Moralia*, or *Moral Essays*, a collection of commentaries on ethical, political, philosophic, scientific, and other issues.

Plutarch's works are valuable in part because he used and quoted from several ancient historical and literary works that were lost in later centuries. Also, he recorded numerous Greek myths in considerable detail. His biography of the Athenian national hero Theseus, for instance, is the most comprehensive known ancient source on that character. In addition, many of Plutarch's moral essays refer to various myths, some famous, others obscure.

Pseudo-Apollodorus

The true identity of this writer, who most likely lived in the first century CE, remains unknown. Modern experts came to call him Pseudo-Apollodorus, meaning "the fake Apollodorus," in reference to an ancient writer of that name who turned out not to have recorded any myths. Whoever he was, he had the distinction of producing what scholars view as the single most valuable surviving ancient collection of myths. Titled the *Bibliotheca*, or

"Library," it is a massive and fascinating work. Among many other tales, it covers the creation of the universe; the emergence of the Titans; the rise of Zeus; Jason's search for the Golden Fleece; the exploits of Heracles, Perseus, and other monster slayers; the founding of Thebes; and the tragic story of Oedipus.

Sophocles

One of the most talented playwrights in history, he was born in Athenian territory in about 496 BCE. His most famous literary achievement is *Oedipus the King*, universally acclaimed as possibly the greatest tragedy ever written. A friend of the Greek historian Herodotus and Athenian statesman Pericles, Sophocles may have served briefly as one of Athens's military generals.

As a playwright, Sophocles relied almost solely on mythology for his themes and plots. In the 123 plays he was said to have written, he repeatedly gave *phone*, or voice, to humans and gods from the legendary Age of Heroes. Among his seven surviving plays, besides *Oedipus the King*, are *Antigone*, *Electra*, and *Oedipus at Colonus*. Most of these works revolve around main characters whose tragic flaws cause them to make mistakes that bring about much suffering and ultimately their own downfalls. After discovering that he unknowingly killed his father and married his mother, for example, Oedipus, king of Thebes, blinds himself and becomes a wandering pauper.

phone

The Greek word for *voice*, from which the word *telephone* derives

SOURCE NOTES

Introduction: Tales That Instilled Fear of the Divine

1. Homer, *Odyssey*, trans. E.V. Rieu. New York: Penguin, 2003, p. 187.
2. Pindar, *Nemean Odes*, in *The Odes of Pindar*, trans. C.M. Bowra. New York: Penguin, 1985, p. 206.
3. C.M. Bowra, *The Greek Experience*. New York: Barnes and Noble, 1996, p. 57.
4. Bowra, *The Greek Experience*, pp. 121–22.
5. Philip Mayerson, *Classical Mythology in Literature, Art, and Music*. Newburyport, MA: Pullins, 2001, p. 280.

Chapter One: Origins of the Greek Myths

6. Plato, *Republic*, in *Great Dialogues of Plato*, trans. W.H.D. Rouse. New York: New American Library, 1956, p. 214.
7. Robert B. Kebric, *Greek People*. Boston: McGraw-Hill, 2005, p. 5.
8. Kebric, *Greek People*, p. 5.
9. Bowra, *The Greek Experience*, p. 32.
10. Michael Grant, *The Rise of the Greeks*. New York: Macmillan, 1987, p. 147.
11. Herodotus, *Histories*, trans. Aubrey de Sélincourt. New York: Penguin, 1996, p. 151.
12. Michael Grant, *Myths of the Greeks and Romans*. New York: Plume, 1995, p. 46.

Chapter Two: Foremost Gods and Goddesses

13. Ovid, *Metamorphoses*, in *Classical Gods and Heroes: Myths as Told by the Ancient Authors*, trans. Rhoda A. Hendricks. New York: Morrow Quill, 1978, p. 79.
14. Quoted in *Homeric Hymn to Demeter*, in *Hesiod, The Homeric Hymns, and Homerica*, trans. Hugh G. Evelyn-White. Cambridge, MA: Harvard University Press, 1964, p. 313.
15. Michael Grant and John Hazel, *Who's Who in Classical Mythology*. New York: Routledge, 2002, p. 157.

Chapter Three: Nature Deities and Other Minor Gods

16. Adrienne Mayor, *The First Fossil Hunters: Paleontology in Greek and Roman Times*. Princeton, NJ: Princeton University Press, 2000, p. 193.
17. Edith Hamilton, *Mythology*. New York: Grand Central, 1999, p. 17.
18. Hesiod, *Theogony*, in *Hesiod and Theognis*, trans. Dorothea Wender. New York: Penguin, 1982, p. 28.
19. Ovid, *Metamorphoses*, trans. A.D. Melville, excerpted in Theoi Greek Mythology, "Phaethon." www.theoi.com.
20. Hesiod, *Theogony*, p. 26.
21. Euripides, *Alcestis*, in *Euripides: Alcestis, Hippolytus, Iphigenia in Tauris*, trans. Philip Vellacott. Baltimore: Penguin, 1968, p. 147.

Chapter Four: Renowned Human Heroes

22. W.H.D. Rouse, *Gods, Heroes and Men of Ancient Greece*. New York: New American Library, 1957, p. 55.
23. Homer, *Iliad*, trans. Robert Fagles. New York: Penguin, 1990, pp. 252–53.
24. Hamilton, *Mythology*, p. 160.
25. Ovid, *Metamorphoses*, trans. Rolfe Humphries. Bloomington: University of Indiana Press, 1967, p. 134.

Chapter Five: Monsters and Other Mythical Beasts

26. Quoted in Alastair Sooke, "The Fantastical Beasts of Ancient Greece," BBC, January 13, 2015. www.bbc.com.
27. Homer, *Odyssey*, Book 17, lines 300–305, 333–335, trans. Don Nardo.
28. Homer, *Odyssey*, trans. W.H.D. Rouse. New York: New American Library, 1937, p. 111.
29. Grant and Hazel, *Who's Who in Classical Mythology*, p. 146.
30. Pseudo-Apollodorus, *Bibliotheca*, trans. Keith Aldrich, excerpted in Theoi Greek Mythology, "Sphinx." www.theoi.com.

Chapter Six: The Major Ancient Myth Tellers

31. Grant, *Myths of the Greeks and Romans*, pp. 154–55.
32. Grant, *Myths of the Greeks and Romans*, p. xvii.
33. Herodotus, *Histories*, p. 425.
34. Hesiod, *Theogony*, p. 41.
35. Aristotle, *Poetics*, trans. Ingram Bywater, in *The Classical Greek Reader*, ed. Kenneth J. Atchity. New York: Oxford University Press, 1996, p. 212.
36. Mary M. Innes, introduction to Ovid, *Metamorphoses*, trans. Mary M. Innes. New York: Penguin, 2006, p. 9.

BY ANOTHER NAME: CHARACTERS OF GREEK AND ROMAN MYTH

The Romans, who had seized control of most of the Greek lands by 146 BCE, became awed by and fascinated with Greek culture. One result was that Rome absorbed and perpetuated Greece's grand corpus of myths but with one small difference: the Romans gave different names to most of the gods and some of the other characters. Although the Romans did not outright copy or borrow the Greek gods, they steadily came to associate many of their own less impressive deities with the usually more majestic Greek ones. For example, over time the somewhat minor Roman sky god Jupiter came to be equated with the stately, immensely powerful Zeus, leader of the Greek pantheon.

Greece	Rome	Role
Aphrodite	Venus	goddess of beauty
Apollo	Apollo	god of prophecy
Ares	Mars	god of war
Artemis	Diana	goddess of the hunt
Asclepius	Aesculapius	god of healing
Athena	Minerva	goddess of wisdom
Cronos	Saturn	father of Zeus/Jupiter
Demeter	Ceres	goddess of plants
Dionysus	Bacchus	god of the vine
Eros	Cupid	god of love
Gaia	Terra	goddess of earth
Hades	Pluto	ruler of the underworld
Helios	Sol	god of the sun
Hephaestos	Vulcan	god of the forge
Hera	Juno	protector of women
Heracles	Hercules	semidivine hero
Hestia	Vesta	goddess of the hearth
Iris	Arcus	goddess of rainbows
Nike	Victoria	goddess of victory
Odysseus	Ulysses	Greek king and hero
Pan	Faunus	god of flocks
Persephone	Proserpina	Hades's queen
Poseidon	Neptune	god of the seas
Prometheus	Prometheus	god of foresight
Rhea	Ops	mother of Zeus/Jupiter
Thanatos	Mors	god of death
Uranus	Caelus	god of the sky
Zeus	Jupiter	leader of the gods

FOR FURTHER RESEARCH

Books

Stephen Fry, *Heroes*. New York: Penguin, 2019.

Annette Giesecke, *Classical Mythology A to Z*. New York: Black Dog and Leventhal, 2020.

Homer, *The Iliad and the Odyssey*, trans. Samuel Butler. Braga, Portugal: Kathartika, 2021.

Lucas Russo, *Uncovering Greek Mythology: A Beginner's Guide into the World of Greek Gods and Goddesses*. Independently published, 2020.

Katerina Servi, *Greek Mythology: Gods & Heroes—the Trojan War and the Odyssey*. Baton Rouge, LA: Third Millennium, 2018.

Internet Sources

Mike Belmont, "Poseidon: Greek God of the Sea," Gods and Monsters, 2020. www.gods-and-monsters.com.

Celeste, "10 Stories from Greek Mythology That Kids Will Love," *Family Experiences Blog*, January 6, 2021. https://familyexperiencesblog.com.

N.S. Gill, "Prometheus: Fire Bringer and Philanthropist." ThoughtCo, March 2, 2019. http://ancienthistory.about.com.

N.S. Gill, "The Ten Greatest Greek Heroes," ThoughtCo, October 23, 2019. http://ancienthistory.about.com.

Hellenic Times, "Beasts of Greek Mythology." www.thehellenictimes.com.

History.com Editors, "Greek Mythology," History.com, October 5, 2020. www.history.com.

Livius.org, "Artemis of Ephesus," April 21, 2019. www.livius.org.

Ohio State University, "Greek Mythology," 2021. https://greekarchaeol ogy.osu.edu.

Nick Romeo, "The Gods of Olympus," *Christian Science Monitor*, 2020. www.csmonitor.com.

Jana Louise Smit, "41 Greek Gods and Goddesses: Family Tree and Fun Facts," History Cooperative, March 31, 2020. https://historycoop erative.org.

Websites
Greek Mythology Link
www.maicar.com
This well-thought-out site has a biographical dictionary with more than six thousand entries and some forty-five hundred photos, drawings, and other images.

Mythweb Encyclopedia of Greek Mythology
www.mythweb.com/encyc
Although not as comprehensive and detailed as Theoi (see below), this website provides a lot of useful information about both major and minor Greek mythological characters.

Theoi Greek Mythology
www.theoi.com
This is unarguably the most comprehensive and reliable general website about Greek mythology on the internet. It features hundreds of separate pages filled with detailed, accurate information, as well as numerous primary sources and reproductions of ancient paintings and mosaics. Highly recommended.

INDEX